Cm. 350/-

D0369193

to the
Bride

OTHER HELEN EXLEY GIFTBOOKS:

My Wedding Planner
Wedding Guest Book
Love Letters
When Love is Forever
A Special Collection in Praise of Mothers
The Love Between Fathers and Daughters

Published simultaneously in 1998 by Exley Publications Ltd in Great Britain,
and Exley Publications LLC in the USA.

2   4   6   8   10   12   11   9   7   5   3   1

Selection and arrangement copyright © Helen Exley 1998.
The moral right of the author has been asserted.

ISBN 1-86187-159-7

Words and pictures selected by Helen Exley.
Pictures researched by Image Select International.
Printed in China.

The Bride is dedicated to Sue, to Leanne and to Sonya (whose work on this book has been so helpful).
Your three lovely weddings inspired me! May your marriages be just as lovely!
The book is also dedicated to Ken and Mer who were married more than sixty years ago
and still inspire me; theirs is the greatest marriage I have ever known – Helen

Exley Publications Ltd, 16 Chalk Hill, Watford, Herts WD1 4BN, UK.
Exley Publications LLC, 232 Madison Avenue, Suite 1206, NY 10016, USA.

EXLEY
NEW YORK • WATFORD, UK

to the
Bride

A HELEN EXLEY GIFTBOOK

Love alone

is capable of uniting human beings

in such a way

as to complete and fulfil them,

for it alone takes them

and joins them

by what is deepest in themselves.

PIERRE TEILHARD DE CHARDIN

(1 8 8 1 - 1 9 5 5)

He called me names of tenderness,
I have never yet heard used to me before —
was bliss beyond belief!
Oh! this was the happiest day of my life!

QUEEN VICTORIA ON HER WEDDING DAY ,
FEBRUARY 10, 1840

This is my lovely day
This is the day I shall remember
the day I'm dying.
They can't take this away
It will be always mine
the sun and the wine,
The seabirds crying.

HERBERT & ELLIS,
FROM "THIS IS MY LOVELY DAY"

I AM LOVED:
A MESSAGE CLANGING
OF A BELL
IN SILENCE.

JOYCE CAROL OATES,
b.1938, FROM "HOW GENTLE"

my life has been so

TO MY BRIDE

*You have given me the highest, completest proof of love
that ever one human being gave another.
I am all gratitude — and all pride
(under the proper feeling which ascribes pride to the right source)
all pride that my life has been so crowned by you.*

ROBERT BROWNING
(1812-1889),
TO ELIZABETH BARRETT

*I will make my kitchen and you shall keep your room
Where white flows the river and bright blows the broom,
And you shall wash your linen and keep your body white
In rainfall at morning and dewfall at night.*

ROBERT LOUIS STEVENSON
(1850-1894),
FROM "ROMANCE"

There shall be
such a oneness between you that when
one weeps,
the other shall taste salt.

PROVERB

I ADD MY BREATH TO YOUR BREATH

THAT OUR DAYS MAY BE LONG ON THE EARTH

THAT THE DAYS OF OUR PEOPLE MAY BE LONG

THAT WE MAY BE ONE PERSON

THAT WE MAY FINISH OUR ROADS TOGETHER

MAY OUR MOTHER BLESS YOU WITH LIFE

MAY OUR LIFE PATHS BE FULFILLED

KERES INDIAN SONG

The bride...

floating all white

beside her father

in the morning

shadow of trees,

her veil flowing

with laughter.

D.H. LAWRENCE

(1885-1930),

FROM "WOMEN IN LOVE"

You

HAVE INTENSIFIED

ALL COLOURS,

HEIGHTENED

ALL BEAUTY,

DEEPENED

ALL DELIGHT.
I LOVE YOU

MORE THAN LIFE,

MY BEAUTY,

MY WONDER.

DUFF COOPER

(1 8 9 0 - 1 9 5 4)

A BETROTHAL

*P*ut your hand on my heart,

     say that you love me as

The woods upon the hills

     cleave to the hills' contours.

     I will uphold you,

     trunk and shoot and flowering sheaf,

And I will hold you,

     roots and fruit and fallen leaf.

E.J. SCOVELL,
b.1907

I will uphold you

come
smiling

Garland your hair with marjoram,

Soft-scented; veil your face and come

Smiling down to us, saffron shoes

On milk-white feet.

Awakened on this happy day,

Join us in lusty marriage-songs,

Join us in dancing, holding high

The marriage-torch.

CATULLUS
(c . 8 4 - c . 5 4 B . C .)

down to us

marriage- songs

This is a joy beyond all other joys —
the day the dream I scarcely dared to dream

comes true.

All happiness is here,

and hope and certainty.

Today we begin to shape a life —

one greater than any

we could have made alone.

PAM BROWN.
b . 1 9 2 8

But when two people are at one

in their inmost hearts,

They shatter even the strength of iron

or bronze.

And when two people understand each other

in their inmost hearts,

Their words are sweet and strong,

like the fragrance of orchids.

I CHING

in their

inmost hearts

It's all I have to bring to-day,

This, and my heart beside,

This, and my heart, and all the fields,

And all the meadows wide.

Be sure you count, should I forget, —

Some one the sun could tell, —

This, and my heart, and all the bees

Which in the clover dwell.

EMILY DICKINSON

(1830-1886)

To be loved and chosen
by a good man
is the best and sweetest thing
which can happen to a woman....

LOUISA MAY ALCOTT

(1832-1888),

FROM "LITTLE WOMEN"

I look at my husband's
beloved body
and I am very aware
of the mystery of the Word
made flesh, his flesh,
the flesh of all of us,
made potential.

MADELEINE L'ENGLE

HIS SMILE IS LIKE SUNSHINE

AND FILLS ME WITH LIGHT.

MIRIAM MAKEBA.

b. 1932

Here all seeking is over,

the lost has been found,

a mate has been found

to share the chills of winter —

now Love asks

that you be united.

Here is a place to rest,

a place to sleep,

a place in heaven.

Now two are becoming one,

the black night is scattered,

the eastern sky grows bright.

At last the great day has come!

HAWAIIAN SONG

That is the true season of love, when
we believe that we alone can love,
that no one could ever have loved so
before us, and no one will love
in the same way after us.

JOHANN WOLFGANG VON GOETHE

(1749-1832)

He gives me the strength that I didn't have,
and I do the same for him.

DEMI MOORE

Love me with thine hand stretched out
Freely — open-minded....

ELIZABETH BARRETT BROWNING

(1806-1861)

no greater magic
in all the world

The sun brings forth the beginning

The moon holds it in darkness

As above, so below

For there is no greater magic in all the world

than that of people joined together in love.

WICCAN BLESSING

Beautiful bride,

to look at you gives joy; your eyes are like honey,

love flows over your gentle face....

SAPPHO
(c . 6 1 2 - 5 8 0 B . C .)

Above all she has given me herself to live for!

Her arms are able to charm away every care;

her words are my solace and inspiration and all because

her love is my life....

THOMAS WOODROW WILSON
(1 8 5 6 - 1 9 2 4) ,
PRESIDENT OF THE UNITED STATES,
TO HIS WIFE ELLEN

*T*o hold her in my arms against the twilight

and be her comrade for ever — this was all

I wanted so long as my life should last....

And this, I told myself with a kind of wonder,

this was what love was:

this consecration, this curious uplifting,

this sudden inexplicable joy, and this

intolerable pain....

ANONYMOUS

*this was all
I wanted*

the birthday

...Raise me a dais of silk and down;

Hang it with vair and purple dyes;

Carve it in doves and pomegranates,

And peacocks with a hundred eyes;

Work it in gold and silver grapes.

In leaves and silver fleurs-de-lys;

Because the birthday of my life

Is come, my love is come to me.

CHRISTINA ROSSETTI

(1830-1874)

I WILL MAKE YOU BROOCHES AND TOYS FOR YOUR DELIGHT

OF BIRD SONG AT MORNING AND STARSHINE AT NIGHT.

I WILL MAKE A PALACE FIT FOR YOU AND ME,

OF GREEN DAYS IN FORESTS AND BLUE DAYS AT SEA.

ROBERT LOUIS STEVENSON
(1850-1894), FROM "ROMANCE"

Come live with me and be my love,

And we will all the pleasures prove

That valleys, groves, hills, and fields,

Woods or sleepy mountain yields.

... And I will make thee beds of roses

And a thousand fragrant posies.

CHRISTOPHER MARLOWE
(1564-1593),
FROM "THE PASSIONATE SHEPHERD TO HIS LOVE"

(i do not know

what it is about you that closes

and opens;only something in me understands

the voice of your eyes is deeper than all roses)

E. E. CUMMINGS

(1 8 9 4 - 1 9 6 2)

How delightful is your love... my bride!
How much more pleasing is your love than wine,
and the fragrance of your perfume than any spice!
Your lips drop sweetness as the honeycomb, my bride;
milk and honey are under your tongue.
The fragrance of your garments is like that of Lebanon.
You are a garden locked up... my bride;
you are a spring enclosed, a sealed fountain.

SONG OF SOLOMON.
4:10,11 (NIV)

Love is the May-day

What woman, however old, has not the bridal favours

and raiment stowed away, and packed in lavender, in the inmost

cupboards of her heart.

WILLIAM MAKEPEACE THACKERAY

(1811-1863)

a person

I don't think I had any concerns when I was walking down the aisle.

I was very happy. It's the culmination of everyone's dream

to find a person you can love who loves you.

TIPPER GORE

of the heart.

BENJAMIN DISRAELI

(1 8 0 4 - 1 8 8 1)

you can love

Now kiss me, my best-dearest beloved!
It seems I am always understood so —
the words are words, and faulty, and inexpressive,
or wrongly expressive, — but when I live under your eyes,
and die, you will never mistake... dearest life of my life,
light of my soul, heart's joy of my heart!...

ROBERT BROWNING
(1812-1889)

After a youth and manhood passed half in unutterable misery
and half in dreary solitude, I have for the first time
found what I can truly love — I have found you.
You are my sympathy — my better self — my good angel.
I am bound to you with a strong attachment.

CHARLOTTE BRONTË
(1816-1855),
FROM "JANE EYRE"

TODAY WE PUT ASIDE THE WORKADAY,

THE ORDINARY, THE DULL ROUTINE.

TODAY WE CELEBRATE.

TODAY WE SET ASIDE THE SENSIBLE, THE PRACTICAL,

THE REASONED ARGUMENT.

TODAY IS A DAY OF DREAMS.

SILK AND RIBBONS, FLOWERS AND CANDLES.

MUSIC. LAUGHTER.

ALL COMBINE TO MAKE THIS YOUR SPECIAL DAY –

THE BEGINNING OF A NEW ADVENTURE.

PAM BROWN,

b . 1 9 2 8

Nothing is sweeter than love;
nothing stronger, nothing higher,
nothing wider;
nothing happier, nothing fuller,
nothing better
in heaven and earth....

THOMAS À KEMPIS
(1 3 7 9 - 1 4 7 1)

There is only one happiness in life, to love and be loved....

GEORGE SAND
(1 8 0 4 - 1 8 7 6)

No cord or cable can draw so forcibly, or bind

so fast, as love can do with a single thread.

ROBERT BURTON
(1 5 7 7 - 1 6 4 0)

Yours is the breath that sets every new leaf aquiver.

Yours is the grace that guides the rush of the river.

Yours is the flush and the flame in the heart of a flower:

Life's meaning, its music, its pride and its power.

ANONYMOUS,
FROM "YOU"

Your words dispel all the care in the world

and make me happy....

They are as necessary to me now

as the sunlight and air....

Your words are my food, your breath my wine —

you are everything to me.

SARAH BERNHARDT
(1844-1923)

human love... consists in this: that two

solitudes protect and border
and greet each other.

RAINER MARIA RILKE (1875-1926)

On whom should I lean, if not on you?
My wary mind turns for refreshment
to the thought of you
as a dusty traveller might sink onto a soft
and grassy bank.

GUSTAVE FLAUBERT
(1821-1880)

Love is to need, and needing, to be needed.
It is the patient architect that builds
Misunderstandings into understanding;
The sunrise, and the waking sea it gilds;
The far new shore, and the precarious landing.

OGDEN NASH
(1902-1971)

A wedding does not depend on flowers or bells or candles, choirs or lace.

It does not need a great congregation

or a vast marquee.

Only two people taking the courage to leave

one life and find another — trusting each other

for true patience, forbearance, strength and love to

face any hardship that the years may bring.

PAM BROWN,
b. 1928

We are today still dizzy
with the astonishment of love.
We are surrounded by affection —
by smiles and kindliness,
by flowers and music, and gifts
and celebration.
Yet they enclose a silence,
where we are close with one another.
My eyes see only you.
I hear nothing but the words
we speak to one another.
This is the day we start our life together.
This is our new beginning.
Our great adventure.

PAMELA DUGDALE

There have been more splendid weddings.

Dresses masterpieces of design,

coronets of pearl and diamond,

shoes as delicate as butterflies.

Flowers flown in from every corner of the world.

Music to stop the heart.

Banquets to amaze the palate.

But better than this one?

Never.

For here are friends and warmth and laughter,

here is shared happiness.

Here is love.

PAMELA DUGDALE

It seems to me, to myself,

that no man was ever before

to any woman what you are to me —

the fulness must be in proportion,

you know to the vacancy...

and only I know what was behind —

the long wilderness without the blossoming rose...

and the capacity for happiness,

like a black gaping hole,

before this silver flooding.

ELIZABETH BARRETT
(1 8 0 6 - 1 8 6 1) ,
TO ROBERT BROWNING
(1 8 1 2 - 1 8 8 9)

strong and

*These rings are gold,
and gold can never tarnish.
Reshape gold and it stays as true.
Whatever changes life may bring
true love survives
— strong and bright and precious.*

PAM BROWN,

b . 1 9 2 8

and precious

bright

With this Ring

I thee wed,

with my body

I thee worship,

and with all my worldly goods

I thee endow.

FROM THE BOOK OF COMMON PRAYER, 1552

I had never been married before;

I don't know if all grooms have the same experience,

but as Kicking Bird began to speak

about what was expected of a Sioux husband,

my mind began to swim in a way that shut out

everything but her: the tiny details of her costume,

the contours of her shape,

the light in her eyes, the smallness of her feet.

I knew that the love between us

would be served.

FROM "DANCES WITH WOLVES"

THAT QUIET MUTUAL GAZE

OF A TRUSTING HUSBAND AND WIFE

IS LIKE THE FIRST MOMENT

OF REST OR REFUGE

FROM A GREAT WEARINESS

OR A GREAT DANGER.

GEORGE ELIOT

(MARY ANN EVANS)

(1819-1880)

mutual gaze

My life, my dear sweet life,
my life-light, my all,
my goods and chattels,
my castles, acres,
lawns and vineyards,
O sun of my life, sun,
moon, and stars,
heaven and earth, my past
and future, my bride,
my girl, my dear friend,
my inmost being,
my heart-blood, my entrails,
star of my eyes,
O dearest,
what shall I call you?

HEINRICH VON KLEIST

(1777-1811)

Today the drab world has been transformed
— decked out with flowers and ribbons.

A feast. A celebration.

Rich with music and laughter, kind thoughts
and recollections.

All in their best
— and you, figures from Romance.

All the world rejoices in a new beginning.

PAM BROWN.

b . 1 9 2 8

I would like to be the air

that inhabits you

for a moment only.

I would like to be that unnoticed

& that necessary.

MARGARET ATWOOD,

b.1939

... I love thee to the depth

and breadth and height

My soul can reach....

I love thee with the breath,

Smiles, tears, of all my life!...

ELIZABETH BARRETT BROWNING

(1806-1861)

We have taken the seven steps. You have become mine forever.

Yes, we have become partners. I have become yours.

Hereafter, I cannot live without you. Do not live without me.

Let us share the joys. We are word and meaning, united.

You are thought and I am sound.

May the nights be honey-sweet for us; may the mornings be honey-sweet for us;

may the earth be honey-sweet for us; may the heavens be honey-sweet for us.

May the plants be honey-sweet for us; may the sun be all honey for us;

may the cows yield us honey-sweet milk!

As the heavens are stable, as the earth is stable, as the mountains are stable,

as the whole universe is stable, so may our union

be permanently settled.

FROM THE HINDU MARRIAGE CEREMONY

$\mathcal{M}$ay your hands
be forever clasped in friendship
and your hearts joined
forever in love.

ANONYMOUS

Two such as you
with such a master speed
Cannot be parted nor be
swept away
From one another once you
are agreed
That life is only life
forevermore
Together wing to wing
and oar to oar.

ROBERT FROST
(1874-1963)

There is no grief,

no sorrow, no despair,

no languor, no dejection,

no dismay,

no absence

scarcely can there be,

for those who love as

we do.

WILLIAM
WORDSWORTH
(1770-1850)

nothing

*L*ove is a great thing, a great good in every way; it alone

lightens what is heavy, and leads smoothly over all roughness.

For it carries a burden without being burdened, and makes

every bitter thing sweet and tasty. Love wants to be lifted up,

not held back by anything low. Love wants to be free,

and far from all worldly desires, so that its inner vision

may not be dimmed and good fortune bind it or misfortune

cast it down. Nothing is sweeter than love....

THOMAS À KEMPIS
(1379-1471),
FROM "THE IMITATION OF CHRIST"

is sweeter, stronger, fuller...

... if you love someone, you need to be with them,
close to them.
You need to be able to confide, to laugh together.
It's just about as important as breathing.

ROSAMUNDE PILCHER,
b.1924

THE SIMPLEST OF VOWS

How strange it is. So much thought, so much concern,

so much anticipation, and yet, now that the moment has come,

how very simple everything is.

We love each other and we need each other. And we believe the only way

this can make a good and full and happy life is in each other's company.

And so we promise to love and honour one another forever.

The simplest and the greatest, perhaps the most demanding of all vows.

CHARLOTTE GRAY,

b. 1937

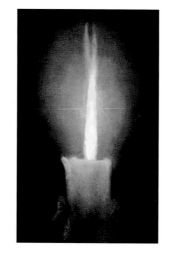

not two human
beings, but one

In a Persian house, there is a wedding mirror,

the breadth of two heads, framed in wrought silver.

This is so because in Persian tradition

it is the union of male and female

which constitutes a human being.

When the new husband and wife gaze into the mirror,

they see in its oval not two human beings, but one.

TERENCE O'DONNELL

Epithalamium

This girl all in white
is my crystal of light
Kissed by heaven to earth in a dancing gift
Of a bride in her freshness, whom youth
and love lift,
With two sunbeams for bridesmaids,
their father's delight

I have married my bride
in a ring of green fields
Round a church on a hill where
all nature's her dress....

all in white

Francis Warner,

from "Epithalamium"

This marriage be wine with halvah, honey dissolving in milk.

This marriage be the leaves and fruit of a date tree.

This marriage be women laughing together for days on end.

This marriage, a sign for us to study.

This marriage, beauty.

This marriage, a moon in a light-blue sky.

This marriage, this silence fully mixed with spirit.

this marriage

JALALU'DDIN RUMI, WRITTEN FOR HIS SON'S WEDDING

To love is to take the greatest risk of all.

It is to give one's future

and one's happiness into another's hands.

It is to allow oneself to trust without reserve.

It is to accept vulnerability.

And thus I love you.

HELEN THOMSON,

b . 1 9 4 3

Let all thy joys be as the month of May,

And all thy days be as a marriage day:

Let sorrow, sickness, and a troubled mind

Be stranger to thee.

FRANCIS QUARLES

AND MAY YOUR DAYS

TOGETHER BE GOOD,

AND LONG UPON THE EARTH.

SYDNEY BARBARA METRICK, FROM

"I DO"

*A*nyone who wants to count
the thousands of joys before you,
the days of delight,
may tally the glittering stars
or go counting sands in the desert.
O Hymen Hymenaee.
Play as you're pleased to.
Be children together and grownups.
And show us some children eventually,
as alive as you two are on this festive day
and at least as good-looking.
So, god of marriage,
we've brought them this far,
and the rest of the song is their singing.
Be good to each other, you two,
and get to work on the singing,
on the labor of loving.
O Hymen Hymenaee, Hymenaee.

CATULLUS
(c. 84 - c. 54 B.C.)

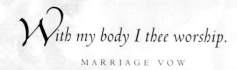
ith my body I thee worship.

MARRIAGE VOW

"SPIRITUAL SURRENDER" IS INTENTIONAL.

IT IS THE RESULT OF THE FREE

AND UNENCUMBERED USE OF ONE'S WILL.

GERALD G. MAY

Two people, yes, two lasting friends.
 The giving comes, the taking ends.
There is no measure for such things.
For this all Nature slows and sings.

ELIZABETH JENNINGS, b.1926,
FROM "FRIENDSHIP"

And throughout all eternity
        I forgive you, you forgive me.

WILLIAM BLAKE (1757-1827)

you forgive me

*The wedding is a fantasy of tulle and icing,
flowers and champagne. A swirl of celebration
round the quiet hub where two people stand alone.
More wise than anyone suspects.
For they know the gown will be laid away,
the cake divided, the roses will fade, the empty bottles will vanish.
There will be flowers and cake, wine and roses in this marriage,
but they will play only a little part in its building and its strength.
Such strange and ordinary things will be the materials
from which this life is made — soap suds and cinnamon buns,
cats and kettles, cups of tea and cauliflowers.
The small anxieties, the great troubles, the petty irritations,
must all be faced and weathered — and the sharing
and the courage and the trust that they will teach
will hold the days together, and build a lifetime.*

PAM BROWN, b. 1928

When two souls,
which have sought each other
for however long in the throng,
have finally found each other,
when they have seen that they are matched,
are in sympathy and compatible,
in a word, that they are alike, there is then
established for ever between them a union,
fiery and pure as they themselves are,
a union which begins on earth and continues
for ever in heaven.
This union is love, true love,
such as in truth very few men can conceive of,
that love which is a religion,
which deifies the loved one, whose life
comes from devotion and passion,
and for which the greatest sacrifices
are the sweetest delights.

VICTOR HUGO
(1802-1885)

Rings are an ancient symbol,
blessed and simple. Round like the sun,
like the eye, like arms that embrace.
Circles, for love that is given
comes back round again and again.
Therefore, may these symbols
remind you that your love, like the sun,
illumines; that your love,
like the eye, must see clearly;
and that your love,
like arms that embrace,
is a grace upon this world.

JAMES FORD, WITH LEIF HASS
AND MARGARET HANDLEY

*I WOULD LIKE TO HAVE ENGRAVED
INSIDE EVERY WEDDING BAND
"BE KIND TO ONE ANOTHER".
THIS IS THE GOLDEN RULE OF MARRIAGE
AND THE SECRET OF MAKING LOVE LAST
THROUGH THE YEARS.*

RANDOLPH RAY,
FROM "MY LITTLE CHURCH AROUND THE CORNER"

You and I
Have so much love
That it
Burns like a fire,
In which we bake a lump of clay
Molded into a figure of you
And a figure of me.
Then we take both of them,
And break them into pieces,
And mix the pieces with water,
And mold again a figure of you,
And a figure of me.
I am in your clay.
You are in my clay.
In life we share a single quilt.
In death we will share one coffin.

KUAN TAO-SHENG
(13TH CENTURY A.D.)

This love is as good
as oil and honey to the throat,
as linen to the body,
as fine garments to the gods,
as incense to worshippers
when they enter in,
as the little seal-ring to my finger.
It is like a ripe pear
in a man's hand,
it is like the dates we mix with wine,
it is like the seeds
the baker adds to bread.
We will be together
even when old age comes.
And the days in between will be food
set before us, dates and honey,
bread and wine.

ANCIENT EGYPTIAN SONG

*W*ho loves the rain

and loves his home,

and looks on life with quiet eyes,

him I will follow

through the storm

and at his hearth-fire

keep me warm.

FRANCES SHAW

so dear I love

So dear I love him,

that with him all deaths

I could endure,

without him live no life.

JOHN MILTON
(1 6 0 8 - 1 6 7 4)

love is all there is

THE TRUTH [IS] THAT THERE IS

ONLY ONE TERMINAL DIGNITY — LOVE.

AND THE STORY OF A LOVE IS NOT IMPORTANT —

WHAT IS IMPORTANT IS THAT ONE IS CAPABLE OF LOVE.

IT IS PERHAPS THE ONLY GLIMPSE WE ARE PERMITTED

OF ETERNITY.

HELEN HAYES,
b . 1 9 0 0

That love is all there is
Is all we know of love.

EMILY DICKINSON
(1 8 3 0 - 1 8 8 6)

I LOVE YOU,
I WILL LOVE YOU

In you are flowers and firelight, stars

and songbirds, the scent of summer,

the stillness just before the dawn.

I love you today, dressed in glory.

I will love you always — dancing, singing,

reading, making, planning, arguing.

I will love you cantankerous and tired,

courageous and in terror,

joyful, fearful and triumphant.

I will love you through all weathers and all change.

For all you are is precious to me.

And every day I live with you and share your love

is a gift to me.

PAM BROWN,
b . 1 9 2 8

EACH BRIDE

MUST SAY TO HER BRIDEGROOM

IN HER HEART

— AND HE TO HER —

I LOVE YOU NOW, THIS MOMENT,

AND FOREVER.

WHEN YOU ARE HANDSOME,

CONFIDENT AND HAPPY —

AND WHEN YOU CANNOT

GET TO SLEEP.

WHEN YOU HAVE WORKED

TOO HARD.

WHEN YOU ARE IN TROUBLE

OR DESPAIR.

I WILL LOVE YOU.

JANE SWAN

To marry is the ultimate act of trust

— to take another's hand and step forward into

the unknown with hope and courage.

CLARA ORTEGA,
b . 1 9 5 5

May all our mistakes and failures

only serve to teach us

how to love each other better.

PETER GRAY,
b . 1 9 2 8

The tapestry is begun.
Here's the start —
a flourishing of flowers and
bells and rings and ribbons.
And now to take
the first bright threads of joy
and stitch them into place.
There is no pattern
you can follow.
Time will hand you silks
and cottons of every hue,
lengths of gold and silver,
knotted darkness.
You must accept them all —
and yet, together,
you can create from them
a wonder, a strength,
a beauty utterly your own.

PAM BROWN,
b. 1928

Now love

starts to learn

patience and forgiveness,

trust and honesty,

unselfishness and

constancy, courage

and sharing.

The threads from which

to weave a marriage.

CHARLOTTE
GRAY,
b . 1 9 3 7

T̲herefore mercifully ordain that we may become aged together.

FROM "THE BOOK OF TOBIT"

To have and to hold from this day forward,

for better for worse, for richer for poorer,

in sickness and in health, to love and to cherish, till death do us part....

FROM THE BOOK OF COMMON PRAYER, 1552

I will follow thee to the last gasp with truth and loyalty.

WILLIAM SHAKESPEARE (1564-1616), FROM "AS YOU LIKE IT"

I would like to go through life side by side with you,

telling you more and more until

we grew to be one being together until the

hour should come for us to die.

JAMES JOYCE (1882-1941)

All these years I have found my pleasures in a thousand things —

and always felt I knew them to the full — but now you open them anew for me.

I see them through your eyes — as well as through my own,

hear them with a new intensity.

The stage is bright, the dance more magical, the trees, the sea, the mountains,

have taken on a new life.

CHARLOTTE GRAY,

b . 1 9 3 7

To love is nothing.
To be loved is something.
To love, and be loved,
is everything.

T. TOLIS V.

TO BE ROOTED IS PERHAPS
THE MOST RECOGNIZED NEED
OF THE HUMAN SOUL.

SIMONE WEIL (1909-1945)

[Love is] born with the pleasure of
looking at each other,
it is fed with the necessity of seeing each other,
it is concluded with the impossibility
of separation!

JOSÉ MARTÍ (1853-1895)

*W*hat greater thing is there
for two human souls
than to feel that they are joined for life —
to strengthen each other in all labour,
to rest on each other in all sorrow,
to minister to each other in all pain,
to be at one with each other
in silent, unspeakable memories
at the moment of the last parting.

GEORGE ELIOT (MARY ANN EVANS)
(1819-1880)

Love bears all things, believes all things,

hopes all things, endures all things.

Love never ends.

I CORINTHIANS 13:7

Until you're a hundred,
Until I'm ninety-nine,
Together
Until white hair grows

JAPANESE FOLK SONG

Through you I drain the pent-up rivers of myself,

In you I wrap a thousand onward years.

WALT WHITMAN
(1819-1892).
FROM "A WOMAN WAITS FOR ME"

Time flies, suns rise, and shadows fall —
Let them go by, for love is over all.

FOUND ON A SUNDIAL

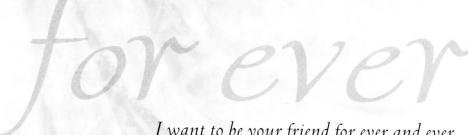

for ever

I want to be your friend for ever and ever.

When the hills are all flat and the rivers are all dry,

when the trees blossom in winter

and the snow falls in summer,

when heaven and earth mix -

not till then will I part from you.

THE YÜEH-FU

Not till the sun excludes you

do I exclude you,

not till the waters refuse to glisten

for you and the leaves to rustle for you,

do my words refuse to glisten and rustle

for you.

WALT WHITMAN (1819-1892)

When I think for one moment
of what the future holds for us together,
what days, and oh, my husband, what nights —
I feel really that I do not belong
to this earth —
it's too small to hold so much.

KATHERINE MANSFIELD
(1 8 8 8 - 1 9 2 3)

the bright stars

Far easier to count each grain of sand
In Africa, or tally the bright stars,
Than reckon up the games of love
You two will play.

CATULLUS
(c . 8 4 - c . 5 4 B . C .)

Above you are the stars

below you are the stones.

As time does pass remember....

Like a star should your love be constant.

Like a stone should your love be firm.

Be close, yet not too close.

Possess one another, yet be understanding.

Have patience each with the other

for storms will come,

but they will go quickly.

Be free in giving of affection

and warmth.

Make love often,

and be sensuous to one another.

Have no fear,

and let not the ways or words

of the unenlightened give you unease.

For the Goddess

and the God are with you.

Now and always.

FROM "PAGAN RITUALS"

*I*nto the enormous sky flew

a whirlwind of blue-gray patches —

a flock of doves spiraling up

suddenly from the dovecotes

*A*nd to see them makes you wish

just as the wedding-feast is ending,

years of happiness for this couple,

flung onto the wind like doves.

BORIS PASTERNAK (1890-1960),
FROM "A WEDDING"

Rising Sun! when you shall shine,
  Make this house happy,
Beautify it with your beams;
  Make this house happy,
God of Dawn! your white blessings spread;
  Make this house happy.
Guard the doorway from all evil;
  Make this house happy.
White corn! Abide herein;
  Make this house happy.
Soft wealth! May this hut cover much;
  Make this house happy.
Heavy Rain! Your virtues send;
  Make this house happy.
Corn Pollen! Bestow content;
  Make this house happy.
May peace around this family dwell;
  Make this house happy.

NAVAJO CHANT

A marriage

makes of two fractional lines a whole;

it gives to two purposeless lives a work,

and doubles the strength of

each to perform it;

it gives to two questioning natures

a reason for living, and something

to live for.

MARK TWAIN
(1 8 3 5 - 1 9 1 0)

$\mathcal{N}$othing in life

is as good as the marriage

of true minds

between man and woman.

As good?

It is life itself.

PEARL BUCK
(1 8 9 2 - 1 9 7 3)

IN THE CONSCIOUSNESS

OF BELONGING TOGETHER,

IN THE SENSE OF CONSTANCY,

RESIDES THE SANCTITY,

THE BEAUTY OF MATRIMONY,

WHICH HELPS US TO ENDURE

PAIN MORE EASILY,

TO ENJOY HAPPINESS DOUBLY,

AND TO GIVE RISE

TO THE FULLEST AND FINEST

DEVELOPMENT OF OUR NATURE.

FANNY LEWALD
(1 8 1 1 - 1 8 8 9)

For one human being
to love another human being:
that is perhaps the most difficult task
that has been entrusted to us,
the ultimate task, the final test and proof,
the work for which all other work
is but preparation....
[Love] is a high inducement
for the individual to ripen,
to become something in [herself]...
to become world in himself
for the sake of another person....

RAINER MARIA RILKE
(1 8 7 5 - 1 9 2 6)

Now you will feel no rain,
For each of you will be shelter to the other.
Now you will feel no cold,
For each of you will be warmth to the other.
Now there is no loneliness for you;
Now there is no more loneliness.
Now you are two persons
But there is one life before you.
Go now to your dwelling place
to enter into the days of your togetherness.

APACHE WEDDING BLESSING

I GAVE THEE
WHAT COULD NOT BE HEARD,
WHAT HAD NOT BEEN GIVEN
BEFORE;
THE BEAT OF MY HEART
I GAVE....

EDITH M. THOMAS

(1 8 5 4 - 1 9 2 5)

ACKNOWLEDGEMENTS

Exley Publications is very grateful to the individuals and organizations who have granted permission to reproduce their pictures. Whilst all reasonable efforts have been made to clear copyright and acknowledge sources and artists, Exley Publications would be happy to hear from any copyright holder who may have been omitted.

A very special thank you to the following for contributing so much to the visual beauty and the sourcing of the pictures in this book: Aisa, AKG London, Alinari, Art Resource, Artworks, Charlotte Augeri, The Board of Trustees of the National Museums and Galleries on Merseyside, The Bridgeman Art Library, Sonya Dougan Furnell, Fine Art Photographic Library, Giraudon, Alex Goldberg, Dora Goldberg, Chris Hutter, The Image Bank, Image Select International, Martin Kerr, The Lynn Tait Gallery, Kurt E. Schon, Sotheby's, Statens Konstmuseer, Superstock, The Telegraph Colour Library, Ronald Tse.

PICTURE CREDITS

Cover and title page: **Signing the Register,** Edmund Blair Leighton (1853-1922), City of Bristol Museum and Art Gallery.

Pages 4/5: **The Wedding Morning,** John A. Bacon, Board of Trustees of the National Museums and Galleries on Merseyside, Lady Lever Art Gallery.

Page 7: **White Roses,** artist unknown.

Pages 8/9: **Serenity,** W.L.Taylor, The Lynn Tait Gallery.

Page 10: **Villa D'Arvray,** Gorot, National Gallery, Washington.

Page 12: **Portrait of a young wife,** Raimundo de Madrazo y Garretta (1841-1920).

Page 14: **Christmas Roses,** © 1998 Gillian Lawson (opposite quote by E.J. Scovell).

Page 17: **Portrait of a woman and her greyhound** (detail), from the English School (19th century), Gavin Graham Gallery, London.

Page 19: **The Artist's Wife at the Hairdresser,** Lovis Corinth (1858-1925), Kunsthalle, Hamburg.

Page 21: **The Wedding Morning** (detail), John A. Bacon, Board of Trustees of the National Museums and Galleries on Merseyside, Lady Lever Art Gallery.

Pages 22/23: **Summer Morning,** © 1998 Charles Courtney Curran (1861-1942), The Cumer Museum of Art and Gardens.

Page 25: **Signing the Register,** Edmund Blair Leighton (1853-1922), City of Bristol Museum and Art Gallery (above quote by Miriam Makeba).

Page 26: **The Wedding Bouquet,** Joanne Gascoigne.

Page 28: **Still Life of White Flowers,** © 1998 Angelina Drumaux (1881-1959), Gavin Graham Gallery, London.

Page 31: **Morning,** S. Koslov.

Page 33: **The Village Wedding,** Sir Luke Fildes (1844-1927), Christies, London.

Page 35: **The Bride,** Anders Zorn (1860-1920), Statens Konstmuseer, Stockholm.

Page 36: **Spring** (detail), © 1998 Sir John Lavery (1856-1941), Musée d'Orsay, Paris.

Page 39: **Portrait of a woman and her greyhound** (detail), from the English School (19th century), Gavin Graham Gallery, London.

Page 40: **Black Bride and Groom,** © 1998 Maria Taglienti (next to quote by e.e. Cummins).

Page 43: **Attending to the Bride,** Joseph Caraud (1821-1905), Waterhouse and Dodd, London.

Page 45: © 1998 Linda Benson

Page 46: **White Roses,** © 1998 Martha Walter (1875-1976), David David Gallery, Philadelphia.

Page 49: **Awaiting The Sailor's Return,** © 1998 David Woodlock (1842-1929).

Pages 50/51: **The Bride,** William Kennedy (1859-1918).

Page 52: **White Roses in a Glass Vase,** © 1998 Albert Williams.

Pages 54/55: **Kasal,** Antonio Mahilum, private collection.

Page 56: **Portrait of a woman and her greyhound,** from the English School (19th century), Gavin Graham Gallery, London.

Pages 58/59: **A Dress Rehearsal,** Albert Chevallier Tayler, National Museums & Galleries On Merseyside.

Page 60: **Reading,** © 1998 Joseph Marius Avy (1871-1939), Whitford & Hughes, London (opposite quote by Elizabeth Barrett).

Page 63: **Accessories for a young bride** (detail), M. Krasowitz.

Pages 64/65: **Solitude,** M. Oliviero.

Page 66: **Roses and Lilies** (detail), Mary Elizabeth Duffield (1819-1914), Victoria and Albert Museum, London.

Page 67: **Betrothed,** W. Savage Cooper.

Page 69: **Till Death Do Us Part** (detail), Edmund Blair Leighton (1853-1922), Forbes Magazine Collection, New York.

Page 71: **Young Girls at the Piano,** Gabriel Deluc, Musée Bonnat, Paris.

Page 72: **The Village Wedding** (detail), Sir Luke Fildes (1844-1927), Christies, London.

Page 75: **The Rising Sun,** Guiseppe Pellizza da Volpedo (1868-1907), National Gallery Of Modern Art, Rome.

Pages 76/77: **The Village Wedding,** Sir Luke Fildes (1844-1927), Christies, London.

Page 78: **Two Roses,** Undated, Juan Luna, private collection.

Page 81: **Marriage of the daughter of Mathias Moreau,** artist unknown, private collection (opposite quote by Charlotte Gray).

Page 82: **Light in the Dark,** Federico D. Estrada, private collection.

Page 85: **Sylvia,** © 1998 Sir Frank Dicksee (1853-1928).

Page 87: **Untitled (trees at night),** Meteyard, Berry Hill Galleries.

Page 88: **Girl reading in an interior,** © 1998 Carl Vilhelm Holsoe (1863-1935), Gavin Graham Gallery, London.

Pages 90/91: **The Wedding Morning,** John A. Bacon, Board of Trustees of the National Museums and Galleries on Merseyside, Isle of Lever Art Gallery.

Page 92: **Scarborough: Sic Transit Gloria Mundi,** John Atkinson Grimshaw (1836-1893), Crescent Art Gallery, Scarborough.

Page 95: **Signing the Register** (detail), Edmund Blair Leighton (1853-1922), City of Bristol Museum and Art Gallery.

Page 96: **Accessories for a young bride,** M. Krasowitz.

Page 99: **In the dining room** (detail), © 1998 Carl Vilhelm Holsoe (1863-1935), Christie's London.

Page 101: **The Measure for the Wedding Ring** (detail), Michael Frederick Halliday (1822-1869) (below quote by Randolph Ray).

Page 102: **Call to Arms** (detail), Edmund Blair Leighton (1853-1922), Roy Miles Gallery.

Page 105: **White Lillies,** Anders Zorn, (1860-1920).

Page 107: **The Wedding,** artist unknown, private collection.

Page 109: **Kasayahan,** Jose W. Hernandez, private collection.

Page 110: **May Morning,** © 1998 Philip Connard (1875-1958), Musée d'Orsay, Paris.

Page 112: **The Wedding of a Matador** (detail), Robert Kemm.

Pages 114/115: **The Wedding Bouquet,** Eugene Bidau.

Page 117: **Signing the Register,** Edmund Blair Leighton (1853-1922), City of Bristol Museum and Art Gallery.

Page 118: **Winter Landscape With Sheep** (detail), Sidney Pike (fl.1880-1907) (opposite quote by Charlotte Gray).

Page 121: **Girl Reading a Letter in an Interior,** © 1998 Peter Ilstedt (1861-1933), Connaught Brown, London.

Page 122: **The Charles V Tapestry,** (detail of the Cardinal blessing the couple), Bruges, Musée du Temps, Besançon.

Page 124: **Roses and Lilies** (detail), Mary Elizabeth Duffield (1819-1914), Victoria and Albert Museum, London.

Page 126: **Technology At Night, Charles River,** Arthur Clifton Goodwin, (1886-1924), The Lowe Art Museum, The University Of Miami.

Page 129: **Roses and Lilies** (detail), Mary Elizabeth Duffield (1819-1914), Victoria and Albert Museum, London.

Pages 130/131: **Moonlight, Isle of Shoals,** © 1998 Frederick Childe Hassam (1859-1935), Christie's Images, New York (opposite quote by Boris Pasternak).

Page 132: **Girl Reading in a Sunlit Room,** © 1998 Carl Vilhem Holsoe (1863-1935).

Pages 134/135: **The River Imatra in Winter,** Gallen Kalella.

Page 137: **Wedding at the Photographer's,** © 1998 Pascal Dagnan-Bouveret (1852-1929), Musée des Beaux-Arts, Lyons.

Page 138: **Dream and Reality,** A. Morbelli.

Page 141: **Spring,** © 1998 Sir John Lavery (1856-1941), Musée d'Orsay, Paris.

Exley Publications are grateful for permission to reproduce copyright material. Whilst every reasonable effort has been made to trace copyright holders, the publishers would be pleased to hear from any not here acknowledged.

CATULLUS: extract from "Roman Epithalamion", adapted by R. Hass from *Into The Garden, A Wedding Anthology* by Robert Hass and Stephen Mitchell. © 1993 Robert Hass and Stephen Mitchell, reprinted by permission of HarperCollins Publishers Inc.

CATULLUS: extract from "Guardian of Helicon...", translated by Frederic Raphael and Kenneth McLeish.

CORINTHIANS 13.7: from the New Testament (circa 54 A.D.). Translated by Catherine Glass, © 1991.

I CHING: translated by Richard Wilhelm. © 1950 Bollingen Foundation Inc., New York. New material © 1967 Bollingen Foundation. Copyright renewed 1977 by Princeton University Press. Reprinted by permission of Princeton University Press.

DUFF COOPER: extract from *A Durable Fire: The Letters of Duff and Diana Cooper*, published by HarperCollins Publishers. © 1983 Artemis Cooper.

E. E. CUMMINGS: from "somewhere i have never travelled gladly beyond" is reprinted from *Complete Poems 1904-1962* by E. E. Cummings, ed. George J. Firmage, by permissions of W. W. Norton & Co. Ltd. © 1991 by the Trustees of the E. E. Cummings Trust and George J. Firmage.

ANCIENT EGYPTIAN SONG: adapted by Robert Hass, from *Into The Garden, A Wedding Anthology* by Robert Hass and Stephen Mitchell. © 1993 Robert Hass and Stephen Mitchell, reprinted by permission of HarperCollins Publishers Inc.

ROBERT FROST: "The Master Speed", from *The Poetry of Robert Frost*, ed. Edward Connery Lathem, published by Jonathan Cape. © 1936, 1964 by Lesley Frost Ballantine, © 1969 by Henry Holt & Co. Inc. Reprinted by permission of Henry Holt & Co. Inc and Random House UK Ltd.

HAWAIIAN SONG: adapted by Jane Hirschfield from *Into The Garden, A Wedding Anthology*, by Robert Hass and Stephen Mitchell, reprinted by permission of HarperCollins Publishers Inc.

HERBERT AND ELLIS: from "This is my Lovely Day", words by Allen Herbert. © 1947 Chappell Music Ltd. Reprinted by permission of International Music Publications Ltd.

VICTOR HUGO: from a letter to Adèle Foucher, translated by Christine Czechowski from *Love Letters* by A. Fraser, published by Weidenfeld & Nicholson, 1976.

THOMAS À KEMPIS: translated by Stephen Mitchell, from *Into The Garden, A Wedding Anthology* by Robert Hass and Stephen Mitchell. © 1993 Robert Hass and Stephen Mitchell, reprinted by permission of HarperCollins Publishers Inc.

OGDEN NASH: from *Loving Letters of Ogden Nash, A Family Album*, published by Little, Brown & Co. Ltd. © 1990 Isabel Nash Eberstadt and Linell Nash Smith.

BORIS PASTERNAK: adapted by R. Hass and S. Mitchell, from *Into The Garden, A Wedding Anthology* by Robert Hass and Stephen Mitchell. © 1993 Robert Hass and Stephen Mitchell, reprinted by permission of HarperCollins Publishers Inc.

JALALU'DDIN RUMI: extract from "This marriage be wine with halvah...", © 1993 Coleman Barks.

E.J. SCOVELL: "A Betrothal", from *Selected Poems*, by E.J. Scovell, © 1991 by E.J. Scovell. Reprinted by permission of Carcanet Press Ltd.

HERMAN SLATER/PAGAN RITUALS: from A Book of Pagan Rituals by Herman Slater (York Beach, ME: Samuel Weiser, 1978). Used by permission of Samuel Weiser.

SONG OF SOLOMON: scripture taken from the Holy Bible, NEW INTERNATIONAL VERSION ®, NIV ®. Copyright 1973, 1978, 1985 by International Bible Society.

KUAN TAO-SHENG: from *The Orchid Boat, Women Poets of China*, translated by Kenneth Roxroth and Ling Chung. Published by McGraw-Hill. © 1972 by K. Roxroth and L. Chung. Reprinted by permission of New Directions Publishing Corp.

FRANCIS WARNER: from "Epithalamium", from *Collected Poems 1960-1984*, published by Colin Smythe.